IT'S TIME TO LEARN ABOUT DALMATIANS

It's Time to Learn about Dalmatians

Walter the Educator

Silent King Books
A WhichHead Entertainment Imprint

Copyright © 2025 by Walter the Educator

All rights reserved. No part of this book may be reproduced in any manner whatsoever without written permission except in the case of brief quotations embodied in critical articles and reviews.

First Printing, 2025

Disclaimer

This book is a literary work; the story is not about specific persons, locations, situations, and/or circumstances unless mentioned in a historical context. Any resemblance to real persons, locations, situations, and/or circumstances is coincidental. This book is for entertainment and informational purposes only. The author and publisher offer this information without warranties expressed or implied. No matter the grounds, neither the author nor the publisher will be accountable for any losses, injuries, or other damages caused by the reader's use of this book. The use of this book acknowledges an understanding and acceptance of this disclaimer.

It's Time to Learn about Dalmatians is a collectible early learning book by Walter the Educator suitable for all ages belonging to Walter the Educator's Collectible Early Learning Book Series. Collect more books at WaltertheEducator.com

USE THE EXTRA SPACE TO TAKE NOTES AND DOCUMENT YOUR MEMORIES

DALMATIANS

Let's meet a dog with spots of black,

It's Time to Learn about
Dalmatians

On shiny fur, both front and back.

So white and clean with dots all 'round

The Dalmatian can't help but stand out proud!

They're tall and strong, with legs so fast,

They run and jump and zoom right past!

They love to play and chase a ball,

And always come when you do call.

Their spots are special, each one neat,

From floppy ears to four quick feet.

No two the same, each dog's unique,

Their look is bold, their style is chic!

When they are born, they have no dots,

Just little pups with creamy spots.

But wait a month or maybe two

The spots will come and peek-a-boo!

It's Time to Learn about
Dalmatians

Dalmatians once ran with fire trucks,

They'd bark and lead, no need for luck.

They cleared the way, so fast, so smart

A brave and loyal dog at heart!

They're great with people, kind and true,

But need good care and exercise too.

They love long walks and time to run,

They shine the most when having fun!

With eyes so bright and tail held high,

They watch the world go walking by.

They like to guard, but not to bite

Unless there's danger late at night!

They're full of energy and cheer,

So keep them close and always near.

They do the best with love and care,

It's Time to Learn about
Dalmatians

And treats and pets and fun to share!

Brushing keeps their short fur clean,

And helps them stay all bright and gleam.

A healthy dog is full of joy

For every girl and every boy.

So if you see those spots so neat,

Marching by on four fast feet

Say hi and smile, don't be shy,

It's Time to Learn about
Dalmatians

A Dalmatian friend is walking by!

ABOUT THE CREATOR

Walter the Educator is one of the pseudonyms for Walter Anderson. Formally educated in Chemistry, Business, and Education, he is an educator, an author, a diverse entrepreneur, and he is the son of a disabled war veteran. "Walter the Educator" shares his time between educating and creating. He holds interests and owns several creative projects that entertain, enlighten, enhance, and educate, hoping to inspire and motivate you. Follow, find new works, and stay up to date with Walter the Educator™

at WaltertheEducator.com